What are...?

FORESTS

Andy Owen
and
Miranda Ashwell

Heinemann
LIBRARY

First published in Great Britain by Heinemann Library
Halley Court, Jordan Hill, Oxford OX2 8EJ
a division of Reed Educational and Professional Publishing Ltd.
Heinemann is a registered trademark of Reed Educational and Professional Publishing Ltd.

OXFORD FLORENCE PRAGUE MADRID ATHENS
MELBOURNE AUCKLAND KUALA LUMPUR SINGAPORE TOKYO
IBADAN NAIROBI KAMPALA JOHANNESBURG GABORONE
PORTSMOUTH NH (USA) CHICAGO MEXICO CITY SAO PAULO

Designed by Susan Clarke
Illustrations by Oxford Illustrators (maps pp.23, 25, 27) and Hardlines (pp.11, 18)
Printed in Hong Kong

02 01 00 99 98
10 9 8 7 6 5 4 3 2 1

ISBN 0 431 02361 1

British Library Cataloguing in Publication Data

What are forests?. – (Heinemann first library)
1. Forests and forestry – Juvenile literature
1. Title II. Ashwell, Miranda III. Forests
333.7'5

Acknowledgements

The Publishers would like to thank the following for permission to reproduce photographs:

Cover photograph: Robert Harding Picture Library

Our thanks to Betty Root for her comments in the preparation of this book.

Every effort has been made to contact copyright holders of any material reproduced in this book. Any omissions will be rectified in subsequent printings if notice is given to the Publisher.

Contents

Some words are shown in bold, **like this**. You can find out what they mean by looking in the Glossary.

Trees and forests

Trees have been growing in this forest for hundreds of years. Wild plants grow under the trees.

This a natural forest.
People did not plant the trees

People use machines to look after these planted trees

These rows of trees were planted by people. The fruit is picked and sold.

Forests in cold places

Pine trees have special leaves called needles. The needles are long, hard and thin. This protects them from the cold and snow.

Pine trees can grow in cold places

Pine trees have been planted
on this cold hill

Farmers cannot grow crops on cold hills.
People plant pine trees instead. Wood
from these trees is sold to make paper,
houses and furniture.

Broadleaved trees

An oak tree in winter

Broadleaved trees have wide leaves that fall off in cold winter weather. The leaves rot into the soil which helps other plants to grow.

The same oak tree in summer

New leaves grow when the weather gets warmer. Sunlight can still reach the plants growing under the tree.

Rainforests

Rainforests are very hot. It rains nearly every day. Hot wet weather means that lots of different plants and trees can grow. Many birds and animals live in the trees.

Trees grow very tall in the rainforests

The top of the trees is called the canopy. Leaves here get the most light

It is much darker under the canopy

The canopy traps the warm, damp air

Young plants grow fast in a race to reach the light. Plants without light will die.

The rainforest **canopy**

Forest fires

Trees become dry and burn easily when there is no rain. Oils in the leaves make the fire very hot.

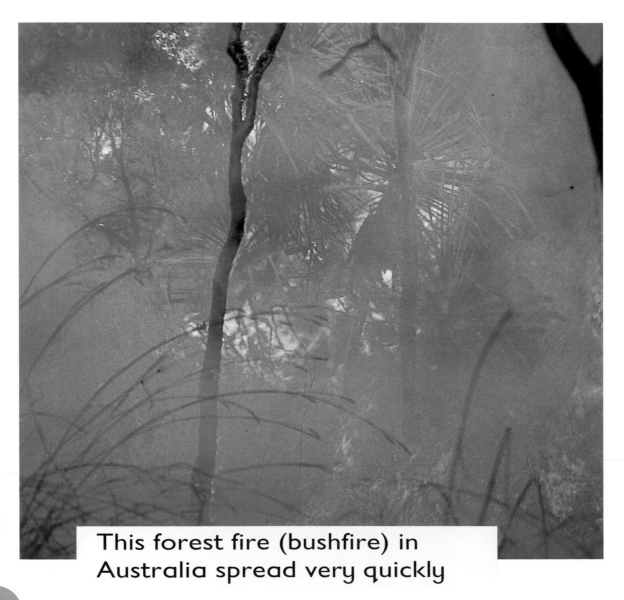

This forest fire (bushfire) in Australia spread very quickly

Some plants are helped by fire. The heat makes some seeds start to grow and the ash makes the soil rich for them.

Some plants grow back quickly after the fire

Mangrove forests

Mangroves are special trees that grow on the coasts of hot countries. Their roots hold the mud together. They protect the land from waves which might wash the mud away.

A young mangrove tree growing in the sea

Mangrove trees grow
in salty sea water

Mangroves have special roots that grow
in the air above the mud. The trees take
in air through these roots.

Cutting down forests

Many trees are cut down
for each road that is built

Some trees take hundreds of years to grow.
It takes only minutes to cut down a tree.

Rainforests are being cut down. Their wood is sold around the world. The animals that live in the forests lose their homes.

Thousands of trees are cut down every day

Washing away the soil

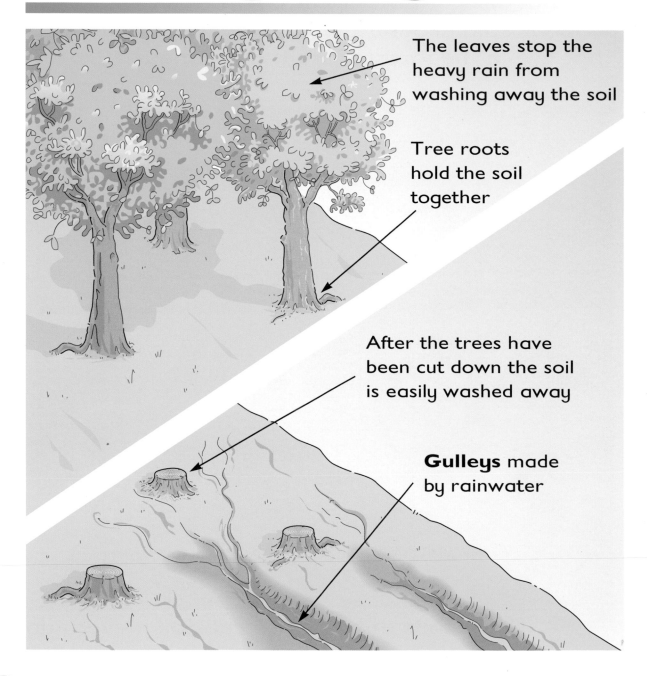

The leaves stop the heavy rain from washing away the soil

Tree roots hold the soil together

After the trees have been cut down the soil is easily washed away

Gulleys made by rainwater

After the trees have been cut down the rain washes away the soil. The flowing water cuts gulleys into the land.

Rain water has made these gulleys

Keeping our trees

Trees need clean air and water. Dirty air can kill trees. We cannot always see this **air pollution** but we can see the damage it does.

Trees are killed by pollution

Planting young trees

We need to plant trees because so many have been cut down. Trees take a long time to grow. It will be many years before they are full grown.

Forest map 1

This photo of the edge of a forest was taken from an aeroplane. Next to the forest are two fields with a hedge in between.

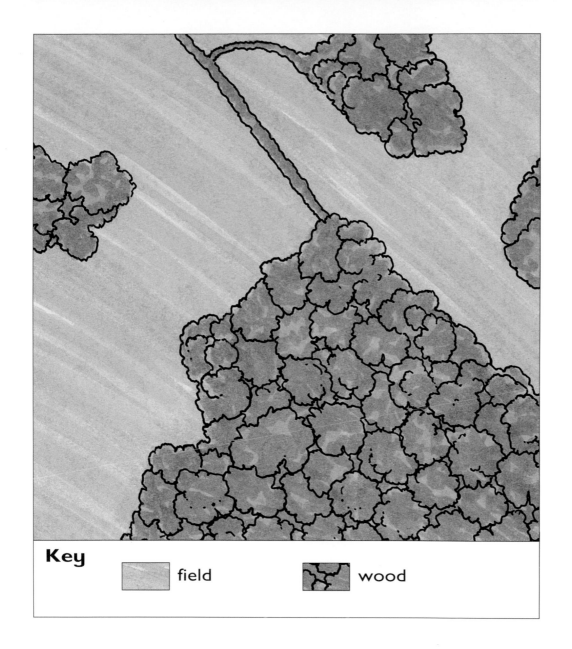

Key

field

wood

This is a map of the same place. The fields are green. The forest is shown using tree shapes.

Forest map 2

This photo is of the same forest. The trees look smaller but you can see more of them. You can also see the edge of a town.

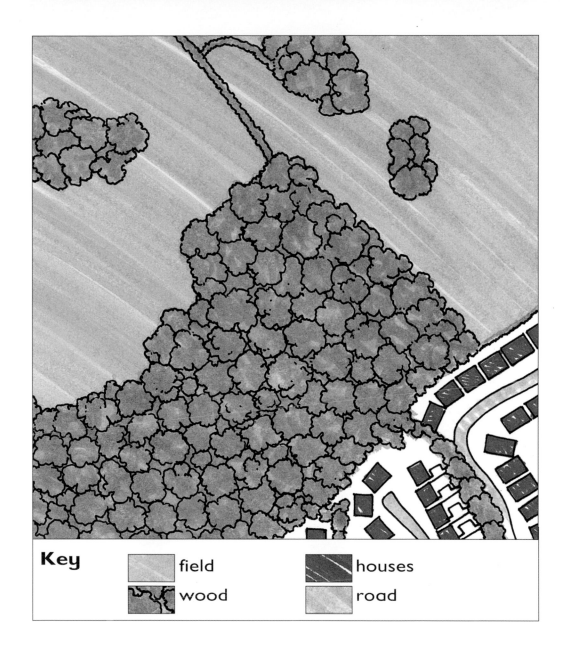

Key

field	houses
wood	road

The forest is still shown using the same tree shapes. Each house is shown on this map.

Forest map 3

You can now see all of the forest. The houses look smaller but you can see more of them. You can also see part of a main road.

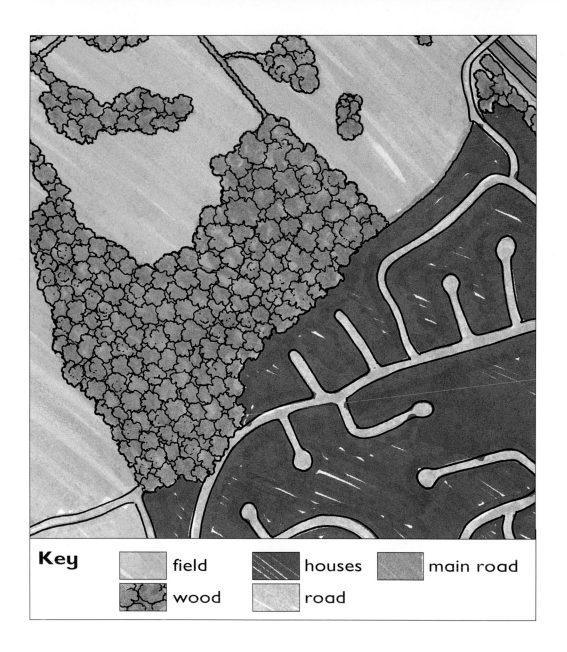

Key

field		houses		main road	
wood		road			

All the forest is shown on the map. There
are too many houses to show each building
so they are shown using a red colour.

Amazing forest facts

The biggest trees in the world are giant redwoods. They grow in North America. Some of them are so big you can drive a car through.

Tree ferns were growing when
dinosaurs were alive. They still grow
in some hot parts of the world.

Glossary

air pollution dirt in the air

broadleaved trees trees that lose their leaves in winter. Another name for a broadleaved tree is deciduous

canopy top of a tree where most leaves grow

gulleys where the ground has been cut by rain water and the soil has been washed away

mangroves trees that grow in warm salty water

pine trees most pine trees keep their leaves all year

rainforests plants and trees growing together in hot wet places

More books to read

Claire Llewellyn. *Why do we have?*
Deserts and Rainforests.
Heinemann, 1997

Rosie McCormick. *World of the Rainforest.*
Two-Can, 1997

Joy Palmer. *First Starts: Rainforests.*
Franklin Watts, 1996

Carole Telford and Rod Theodorou.
Amazing Journeys: Up a Rainforest Tree.
Heinemann, 1997

Index